What is Contemplation?

WHAT IS CONTEMPLATION? BY THOMAS MERTON

Templegate Publishers
Springfield, Illinois

First published in 1950
© 1978 The Trustees of the Merton Legacy Trust

ISBN: 87243-103-7

Templegate Publishers
P.O. Box 5152, 302 East Adams Street
Springfield, Illinois 62705

Revised edition 1981

WHAT IS CONTEMPLATION?

There are so many Christians who do not appreciate the magnificent dignity of their vocation to sanctity, to the knowledge, love and service of God.

There are so many Christians who do not realize what possibilities God has placed in the life of Christian perfection — what possibilities for joy in the knowledge and love of Him.

There are so many Christians who have practically no idea of the immense love of God for them, and of the power of that Love to do them good, to bring them happiness.

Why do we think of the gift of contemplation, infused contemplation, mystical prayer, as something essentially strange and esoteric reserved for a small class of almost unnatural beings and prohibited to everyone else? It is perhaps because we have forgotten that contemplation is the work of the

Holy Ghost acting on our souls through His gifts of Wisdom and Understanding with special intensity to increase and perfect our love for Him. These gifts are part of the normal equipment of Christian sanctity. They are given to all in Baptism, and if they are given it is presumably because God wants them to be developed. Their development will always remain the free gift of God and it is true that His wise Providence sees fit to develop them less in some saints than in others. But it is also true that God often measures His gifts by our desire to receive them, and by our cooperation with His grace, and the Holy Spirit will not waste any of His gifts on people who have little or no interest in them.

It would be a great mistake to think that mystical contemplation necessarily brings with it a whole litany of weird phenomena — ecstasies, raptures, stigmata and so on. These belong to quite a different order of things. They are "charismatic" gifts, *gratiae gratis datae*, and they are not directly ordered

to the sanctification of the one who receives them. Infused contemplation, on the contrary, is a powerful means of sanctification. It is the work of love and nothing is more effective in increasing our love for God. In fact, infused contemplation is intimately connected with the pure and perfect love of God which is God's greatest gift to the soul. It is deep and intimate knowledge of God by a union of love — a union in which we learn things about Him that those who have not received such a gift will never discover until they enter heaven.

Therefore, if anyone should ask, "Who may desire this gift and pray for it?" the answer is obvious: *everybody*.

But there is only one condition. If you desire intimate union with God you must be willing to pay the price for it. The price is small enough. In fact it is not even a price at all: it only seems to be so with us. We find it difficult to give up our desire for things that can never satisfy us in order to purchase the One Good in Whom is all our joy

— and in Whom, moreover, we get back everything else that we have renounced besides!

The fact remains that contemplation will not be given to those who willfully remain at a distance from God, who confine their interior life to a few routine exercises of piety and a few external acts of worship and service performed as a matter of duty. Such people are careful to avoid sin. They respect God as a Master. But their heart does not belong to Him. They are not really interested in Him, except in order to insure themselves against losing heaven and going to hell. In actual practice, their minds and hearts are taken up with their own ambitions and troubles and comforts and pleasures and all their worldly interests and anxieties and fears. God is only invited to enter this charmed circle to smooth out difficulties and to dispense rewards.

THE PROMISES OF CHRIST

The Discourse of Our Lord Jesus Christ at the Last Supper, His spiritual testament, was a summary of the whole spiritual life. It laid the foundations of all mystical theology and defined Christian perfection.

He promised to His disciples (and to us through them) the greatest of all gifts. He promised them that Spirit Who is infinite, uncreated Love, the Love Who is God Himself and Who proceeds from God the Father and the Son and unites them in a bond of infinite charity which is their own Nature hypostatized as their Gift to One Another.

"The Spirit of Truth whom the world cannot receive because it seeth Him not, nor knoweth Him: *but you shall know Him;* because He shall abide with you and be in you." (John xiv, 17.)

"The Holy Ghost, whom the Father

will send in my name, *will teach you all things.*" (Ibid. 26.)

Through that Spirit the Father and the Son will both reveal themselves to us, and we will know and love them:

"He that loveth me shall be loved of my Father: and *I will love him and will manifest myself to him . . . My Father will love him and we will come to him and make our abode with him.*" (Ibid. 21 and 23.)

But such knowledge and love, infused into our hearts by the God of love manifesting Himself to us, is essentially the same beatitude as the blessed enjoy in heaven. "For this is eternal life: That they may know Thee the only true God, and Jesus Christ whom Thou hast sent." (Ibid. xvii, 3.)

Is it any wonder that this intimate knowledge of the Holy Trinity and of Jesus, the Incarnate Word, should open up infinite depths of joy and peace to the contemplative Christian soul?

"These things I have spoken to you *that my joy may be in you, and your joy may be filled.*" (Ibid. xv, 11.)

"Peace I leave with you, *my peace I give you. Not as the world giveth do I give unto you . . ."* (Ibid. xiv, 27.)

The joy of the contemplative is consummated in perfect union:

"The glory which Thou hast given to me I have given them; that they may be one as we also are one: I in them and Thou in me, that they may be made perfect in one." (Ibid. xvii, 22, 23.)

The seeds of this perfect life are planted in every Christian soul at Baptism. But seeds must grow and develop before you reap the harvest. There are thousands of Christians walking about the face of the earth bearing in their bodies the infinite God of Whom they know practically nothing.

The seeds of contemplation and sanctity have been planted in those souls, but they merely lie dormant. They do not germinate. They do not grow. In other words: sanctifying grace occupies the substance of their souls but never flows out to inflame and irrigate and take possession of their faculties, their intellect and will. *God does not manifest Himself to these souls because they do not seek Him with any real desire.*

They are men divided between God and the world. They allow God to maintain His rights over the substance of their souls, but their thoughts and desires do not belong to Him. They belong to the world and to external things. Consequently, as far as their knowledge of God is concerned, these Christians are in the same condition as the men of this world. For them, too, the Spirit of Truth cannot be received "because they see Him not, nor know Him." For them too it must be said: "The sensual man perceiveth not these things that are of the Spirit of God: for it is foolishness to him and he cannot understand." (I Cor. ii, 14.)

ST. THOMAS AQUINAS

In His discourse at the Last Supper Jesus promised the Holy Ghost, with His contemplative gifts. But the promise was accompanied by a denial. The Holy Ghost would be given to those who would receive Him. To those who would not receive Him, He would be denied.

St. Thomas Aquinas, commenting on the words of St. John's Gospel (ch. xiv), explains the difference between the two.

Contemplation will be denied to a man in proportion as he belongs to the world. The expression "the world" signifies those who love the things of this world. They cannot receive the Holy Spirit Who is the Love of God. As St. John of the Cross says: "Two contraries cannot coexist at the same time in the same subject."

If a man wants to prepare himself

to receive the Holy Ghost and His Love, he must withdraw his desires from all the satisfactions and interests this world has to offer, for spiritual things cannot be appreciated or understood by the mind that is occupied with temporal and merely human satisfactions. *Spiritualia videri non possunt nisi quis vacet a terrenis.*

The Angelic Doctor explains that the Holy Ghost does not manifest Himself to worldly men because *they do not desire to know Him.* They are content to occupy their minds with lower things. But desire is the most important thing in the contemplative life. Without desire we will never receive the great gifts of God. *Dona spiritualia non accipiuntur nisi desiderata.* St. Thomas adds: *nec desiderantur nisi aliqualiter cognita.* There can be no desire where there is not at least a little knowledge. We cannot desire union with God unless we know that such a union exists and have at least some idea of what it is.

But the worldly man, and the

Christian who is entirely concerned with his activities and temporal interests, not only does not desire contemplation but he even makes himself incapable of knowing what it is. The only way to find out anything about the joys of contemplation is *by experience.* We must taste and see that the Lord is sweet. *Gustate et videte quoniam suavis est Dominus.*

St. Thomas says that worldly men have lost that sense of taste for spiritual things. "As the tongue of a sick man cannot taste good things . . . so the soul infected with the corruption of the world has no taste for the joys of heaven."

In what does this taste consist? *It is love.*

Jesus Himself made it quite clear that the one thing on which the spiritual life depends is *love.*

"If you love me . . . I will ask the Father and He will give you another Paraclete . . . *He that loveth me* shall be loved of my Father and *I will love him and manifest myself to him . . . "* (John xiv, 15 and 21.)

And He added the final, perfect test, the proof of true love and the one decisive factor which distinguishes the contemplative from the man of the world, the saint from the mediocre Christian. *"If anyone love me he will keep my word."* (Ibid. 23, 24.)

It is really this total and uncompromising docility to the will of God that gives a man a taste for spiritual things. It is this delicate instinct to yield to the slightest movement of God's love that makes the true contemplative. As St. Thomas says:

Per obedientiam homo efficitur idoneus ad videndum Deum.

"It is obedience that makes a man fit to see God."

KINDS OF CONTEMPLATION

There is really only one kind of contemplation. The word, used properly, in its strict and correct sense signifies infused or mystical contemplation. This is also called "passive" contemplation. It is a pure gift of God and, as we shall see, God is the principal agent Who infuses it into the soul and Who, by this means, takes possession of the soul's faculties and moves them directly according to His will.

ACTIVE CONTEMPLATION

There is another, broad sense of the word contemplation. Here the soul, aided by ordinary grace, works in the familiar natural mode. One reasons and uses one's imagination and elicits affections in the will. One makes use of all the resources of theology and philosophy and art and music in order to focus a simple affective gaze on

God. All the traditional means and practices of the interior life come under the heading of *active contemplation* to the extent that they help us to know and love God by a simple gaze on Him.

Active contemplation then demands thought and action and acts of will. Its function is to awaken and prepare the mind, to turn the heart towards God, to arouse a desire to know God better and to rest in Him. It introduces the soul to the joys of the spiritual life. It gives him a healthy taste for the things of the supernatural order and weans him away from the satisfactions of the body and of merely natural knowledge.

Above all, active contemplation prepares the way for love. It teaches obedience and humility. It shows a man how to seek God in His will. It makes the soul attentive to God's presence and His desires. It teaches one to think about God instead of about the world, to desire to please God rather than to enjoy the satisfactions of the world. It shows us how to trust God and leads us on to abandon ourselves more and

more to Him.

Passive contemplation is not demanded of all Christians. But at least *some* active contemplation would appear to be, in practice if not in theory, *absolutely essential to a truly Christian life.*

LITURGY ✖

The liturgy teaches active contemplation above all by its rich content of theology and scriptural revelation, which it surrounds with art and music and poetry of chaste and austere power, deeply affecting to any soul that has not had its taste perverted by the artistic fashions of a degenerate age.

But at the same time the liturgy tends to bring the soul to passive or infused contemplation by the power of that great central action, the Mass, in which Christ lives on in the world and in time and by which He draws all things to Himself.

It is in the Mass that we are united to Christ from Whom all the graces of prayer and contemplation flow. Indeed, Jesus is Himself the very embodiment of contemplation — a human nature united in one Person with the infinite Truth and Splendour of God. We become contemplatives to the extent that we participate in Christ's Divine Sonship, and that participation is granted to us in a special way in Holy Mass.

And so, at the Last Supper, Jesus gave us more than a sublime doctrine: He gave us Himself, "the way, the truth and the life." The Blessed Sacrament is not a sign or a figure of contemplation; it contains Him Who is the beginning and end of all contemplation. It should not be surprising then that one of the most normal ways of entering into infused prayer is through the graces given in Holy Communion.

UNION WITH GOD IN ACTIVITY

The great majority of Christians will never become pure contemplatives on earth. But that does not mean that those whose vocation is essentially active must resign themselves to being excluded from all the graces of a deep interior life and all infused prayer. Christ has promised that the Three Divine Persons will manifest themselves *to all who love Him*. There are many Christians who serve God with great purity of soul and perfect self-sacrifice in the active life. Their vocation does not allow them to find the solitude and silence and leisure in which to empty their minds entirely of created things and to lose themselves in God alone. They are too busy serving Him in His children on earth. At the same time, their minds and temperaments do not fit them for a purely contemplative life: they would know no peace without exterior activity. They would not know what to do with themselves. They would vegetate and *their interior life would grow cold*. Nevertheless they know how to find God by devoting themselves to Him in self-sacrificing labours in which they are able to remain in His presence all day long. They live and work in His company. They realize that He is within them and they taste deep, peaceful joy in being with Him. They lead lives of great simplicity in which they do not need to rise above the ordinary levels of vocal and affective prayer. Without realizing it, their humble prayer is, for them, so deep and interior that it brings them to the threshold of contemplation. They never enter deeply into the contemplative life but they are not unfamiliar with graces akin to contemplation. Although they are active labourers they are also *quasi-contemplatives* because of the great purity of heart maintained in them by obedience, fraternal charity, self sacrifice and perfect abandonment to God's will in all that they do and suffer. They are much closer to God than they realize. They enjoy a kind of "masked" contemplation.

Such Christians as these, far from being excluded from perfection, may reach a higher degree of sanctity than others who have been apparently favored

Angels leaving
a Hill.

with a deeper interior life. Yet there is all the difference in the world between these quasi-contemplatives and the surface Christian whose piety is merely a matter of externals and formal routine. The difference is: *these men live for God and for His love alone.* They cannot help knowing something about Him.

INFUSED CONTEMPLATION

In the strict sense of the word, CONTEMPLATION IS A SUPERNATURAL LOVE AND KNOWLEDGE OF GOD, SIMPLE AND OBSCURE, INFUSED BY HIM INTO THE SUMMIT OF THE SOUL, GIVING IT A DIRECT AND EXPERIMENTAL CONTACT WITH HIM.

Mystical contemplation is an intuition of God born of pure love. It is a gift of God that absolutely transcends all the natural capacities of the soul and which no man can acquire by any effort of his own. But God gives it to the soul in proportion as it is clean and emptied of all affections for things outside of Himself. In other words, it is God manifesting Himself, according to the promise of Christ, to those who love Him. Yet the love with which they love Him is also His gift; we only love Him because He has first

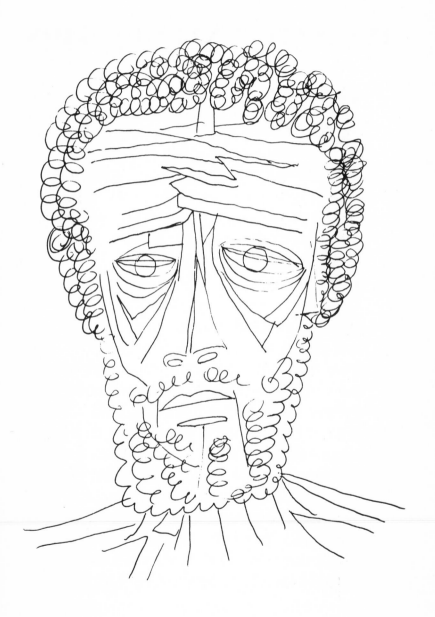

loved us. *Ipse prior dilexit nos.*

But the thing that must be stressed is that *contemplation is itself a development and a perfection of pure charity.* He who loves God realizes that the greatest joy, the perfection of beatitude is to love God and renounce all things for the sake of God alone — or for the sake of love alone because God Himself is love. Contemplation is an intellectual experience of the fact that God is infinite Love, that He has given Himself to us, and that from henceforth, love is all that matters.

ST. BERNARD OF CLAIRVAUX

The great Cistercian theologian of the twelfth century remarks that love is sufficient to itself, is its own end, its own merit, its own reward. It seeks no cause beyond itself and no fruit outside itself. The very act of loving is the greatest reward of love because to love with a pure, disinterested love the God Who is the supreme object of all love can only be the purest and most perfect

joy and the greatest of all rewards.
*Amor praeter se non requirit causam,
non fructum: fructus ejus, usus ejus.*
And he exclaims: "I love simply
because I love, and I love in order to
love." *Amo quia amo, amo ut amem.*
(Serm. 83 in Cantica.)

"A RAY OF DARKNESS"

From what has been said, one might
get the idea that infused contemplation
is all sweetness and understanding and
consolation and joy. *It is true that the
presence of God in contemplation
always brings peace and strength to the
soul,* but sometimes that peace is
almost buried under pain and darkness
and aridity. Strength is given to us,
sometimes, only when we have been
reduced to an extreme sense of our own
helplessness and incapacity.

Do not think that contemplation,
especially in the beginning, brings you
a clear, definite knowledge of God. Do
not think that your love will always be
inflamed to strong, consoling acts that

fly to God with great facility. Do not think that your soul will always be lifted up to Him in lightness and liberty and joy.

Contemplation is the light of God playing directly upon the soul. But every soul is weakened and blinded by the attachment to created things, which it tends to love inordinately by reason of original sin. Consequently, the light of God affects that soul the way the light of the sun affects a diseased eye. It causes *pain*. God's love is too pure. The soul, impure and diseased by its selfishness, is shocked and repelled by the very purity of God. It cannot understand the suffering caused by the light of God. It has formed its own ideas of God: ideas that are based upon its natural knowledge and which unconsciously flatter its own self-love. But God contradicts those ideas. His light denies and defeats all the human and natural notions the soul has formed for itself concerning Him. The experience of God in infused contemplation is a flat contradiction of all the soul has imagined concerning Him. The fire of His infused love launches a merciless attack upon the self-love of the soul attached to human consolations and to those lights and feelings which it required as a beginner, but which it falsely imagined to be the great graces of prayer.

Infused contemplation, then, sooner or later brings with it a terrible interior revolution. Gone is the sweetness of prayer. Meditation becomes impossible, even hateful. Liturgical functions seem to be an insupportable burden. The mind cannot think. The will seems unable to love. The interior life is filled with darkness and dryness and pain. The soul is tempted to think that all is over and that, in punishment for its infidelities, all spiritual life has come to an end.

This is a crucial point in the life of prayer. It is very often here that souls, called by God to contemplation, are repelled by this "hard saying," turn back and "walk no more with Him." (John vi, 61-67.) God has illuminated

their hearts with a ray of His light. But because they are blinded by its intensity it proves to be, for them, *a ray of darkness.* They rebel against that. They do not want to *believe* and remain in obscurity: they want to *see.* They do not want to walk in emptiness, with blind trust: they want to know where they are going. They want to be able to depend on themselves. They want to trust their own minds and their own wills, their own judgments and their own decisions. They want to be their own guides. They are therefore sensual men, who "do not perceive the things that are of the Spirit of God." To them, this darkness and helplessness is foolishness. Christ has given them His Cross and it has proved to be a scandal. They can go no further.

Generally they remain faithful to God: they try to serve Him. But they turn away from interior things and express their service in externals. They externalize themselves in pious practices, or they immerse themselves in work in order to escape the pain and sense of defeat they have experienced in what seems, to them, to be the collapse of all contemplation.

The light shineth in darkness and the darkness did not comprehend it. (John i, 5.)

THE TEST

General principles are only useful when they are applied to individual cases. Dryness in meditation, helplessness in the struggle for virtue are no sure indication, by themselves alone, that contemplation has begun. Each individual case must be decided on its own merits, in the light of circumstances. Aridity and helplessness in the interior life may be the result of sin or infidelity, or simply an expression of laziness. This is all the more likely if the soul has *never* been able to meditate and has *never* experienced any sensible fervour at any time. Then too these difficulties may spring from bad health and nothing more.

There is a true test of infused contemplation. This test is that there will always be a *positive element in it,* no matter how negative it may at first seem. Underneath the suffering, behind the curtain of darkness, beyond the pain, one can find sure and positive signs that God is at work. These signs will make it probable that the trials are a purification belonging to the order of infused prayer.

PEACE, RECOLLECTION, AND DESIRE

Let us suppose that a soul once able to meditate and produce fervent affections of love for God in the human way is now no longer able to do so, but seeks Him in aridity, darkness and frustration. What is its deepest instinct at that time? Does it resign itself to remaining in the cloud of obscurity which it cannot penetrate? Does it find peace in abandoning itself to God's will? Is it content to rest in pure faith and blind hope? Does the attempt to meditate and reason and produce affections rob it of peace and throw it into confusion and disgust, while a simple attitude of patient waiting in darkness restores order and harmony to the soul? This would help

to decide that God wanted to lead such a one by the ways of infused prayer. By itself it does not settle the case conclusively.

If, however, the soul that is thus led into darkness discovers there deep recollection and finds that the worries and cares of the world and of material things fall into background — even though distractions may continue to plague it against its desire — this also would be an argument in favour of infused prayer. And this will be all the more true if the attempt to meditate and produce acts robs the soul of recollection and throws it into a turmoil.

Finally, the surest sign of infused contemplation behind the cloud of darkness is a *powerful, mysterious and yet simple attraction which holds the soul prisoner in this darkness and obscurity*. Although the soul is filled with a sense of affliction and defeat, *it has no desire to escape from this aridity*. Far from being attracted by the legitimate pleasures and lights and relaxations of the natural order, it finds them repellent. All created goods only make it restless. They cannot satisfy it. *But at the same time there is a growing conviction that joy and peace and fulfillment are only to be found somewhere in this lonely night of aridity and faith.*

Sometimes this attraction is so powerful that it cancels out all the suffering felt by the soul, which counts its own pain and helplessness as nothing and becomes totally absorbed in this inexplicable desire for peace which it thinks can somehow be found in this solitude and darkness. It follows the attraction, or rather allows itself to be drawn through the night of faith by the power of an obscure love which it cannot yet understand.

Then suddenly comes the awakening.

The soul one day begins to realize, in a manner completely unexpected and surprising, that in this darkness it has found the living God. It is over-whelmed with the sense that He is there and that His love is surrounding and absorbing it on all sides. At that instant, there is no other important reality but God, infinite Love. Nothing else matters. The darkness remains as dark as ever and yet, somehow, it seems to have become brighter than the brightest day. The soul has entered a new world, a world of rich experience that transcends the level of all natural knowledge and all natural love.

From then on its whole life is transformed. Although externally sufferings and difficulties and labours may be multiplied, the soul's interior life has become completely simple. It consists of one thought, one love: GOD ALONE. In all things the eyes of the soul are upon Him. He has become everything. And this gaze of the soul includes in itself all adoration, all petition; it is continual sacrifice, it offers God unceasing reparation. It is pure and simple love, that love which, as St. Bernard says, draws and absorbs every other activity of the soul into itself: *Amor caeteros in se omnes traducit et captivat affectus.* (Serm. 83 in Cantica.) This love, infused into the soul by God, unifies all its powers and raises them up to Him, separating its desires and affections more and more from the world and from perishing things. Without realizing it, the soul makes rapid progress and becomes adorned with many virtues: but it does not consider itself. It has no eyes for anything or anyone but God alone.

It has entered into the maturity of the spiritual life, the illuminative way, and is being drawn on towards complete union with God, in which sanctity and true Christian perfection are found.

WHAT TO DO — THE TEACHING OF ST. JOHN OF THE CROSS

St. John of the Cross, one of the greatest as well as the safest mystical theologians God has given to His Church, explains in great detail how the soul should behave in order to accept this beautiful gift of God and make use of it without spoiling His work. It is very important to have competent guidance and instruction in the ways of contemplative prayer. Otherwise it will be almost impossible to avoid errors and obstacles. The reason for this is that no matter how good the intentions of the soul may be, its natural coarseness and clumsiness still prevent it from sensing the full import of the delicate work performed by God's love within its most intimate depths and cooperating with His action.

The most important thing of all is to get some realization of what God is doing in your soul. Learn the tremen-

dous value of this obscure and sometimes crucifying light of faith which
darkens and empties your mind with
respect to all natural convictions and
leads you into realms without evidence
in order to bring you to the threshold
of an actual experimental contact with
the living God. In fact, St. John of the
Cross does not hesitate to say that this
darkness is caused by the presence of
God in the intellect, blinding our finite
powers by the brightness of His
unlimited actuality and truth.

"This Dark Night *is the
inflowing of God into the soul which
purges it* of its ignorances and
imperfections, natural and spiritual,
and which is called by contemplatives
infused contemplation. . . *Herein God
secretly teaches the soul and instructs
it in perfection of love without its
doing anything or understanding of
what manner is this infused
contemplation.*"
(Dark Night, II, v, 1.)

Solemn Assizes

And so you will see that in order to cooperate with this great work of grace in your soul you must not desire or seek the things which God's immense light is striving to drive out of you, that He may replace them by His own truth. Do not therefore lament when your prayer is empty of all precise, rational knowledge of God and when you cannot seize Him any longer by clear, definite concepts. Do not be surprised or alarmed when your will no longer finds sweetness or consolation in the things of God and when your imagination is darkened and thrown into disorder. You are out of your depth; your mind and will have been led beyond the borders of the natural order and they can no longer function as they used to because they are in the presence of an object that overwhelms them. This is precisely as God wants it to be, for He Himself is that object and He is now beginning to infuse into the soul His own Light and His own Love in one general confused experience of mute attraction and peaceful desire. Do not seek anything more precise than this for the moment. If you attempt by your own action to increase the precision of your knowledge of God or to intensify the feeling of love you will interfere with His work and He will withdraw His light and His grace, leaving you with the fruit of your own poor natural activity.

The natural appetite of your mind and will for their own particular kind of satisfaction will suffer and rebel against this seemingly hard regime: but remember as the saint says: *"By means of this dark and loving knowledge God is united to the soul in a lofty and divine degree.* For this dark and loving knowledge which is faith serves as a means to divine union in this life even as in the next life the light of glory serves as an intermediary to the clear vision of God."* (Ascent of Mount Carmel, ii, 24.)

Do not, then, stir yourself up to useless interior activities. Avoid everything that will bring unnecessary complications into your life. Live in as much peace and quiet and retirement as you can, and do not go out of your way to get involved in labours and duties no matter how much glory they may seem to give to God. Do the tasks appointed to you as perfectly as you can with disinterested love and great peace in order to show your desire of pleasing God. Love and serve Him peacefully and in all your works preserve recollection. Do what you do quietly and without fuss. Seek solitude as much as you can, dwell in the silence of your own soul and rest there in the simple and simplifying light which God is infusing into you. Do not make the mistake of aspiring to the spectacular "experiences" that you read about in the lives of the great mystics. None of those graces (called *gratis datae*) can sanctify you nearly as well as this obscure and purifying light and love of God which is given you to no other end than to make you perfect in His love. "Passing beyond all that can be known and understood both spiritually and naturally, *the soul will desire with all desire to come to that* WHICH CANNOT BE KNOWN NEITHER CAN ENTER INTO ITS HEART. And leaving behind *all that it experiences and feels both temporally and spiritually* and all that it is able to experience in this life, IT WILL DESIRE WITH ALL DESIRE TO COME TO THAT WHICH SURPASSES ALL FEELING AND EXPERIENCE." (Ascent of Mount Carmel, ii, 3.)

Do not be too anxious about your advancement in the ways of prayer, because you have left the beaten track and are traveling by paths that cannot be charted and measured. Therefore leave God to take care of your degree of sanctity and of contemplation. If you yourself try to measure your own progress you will waste your time in futile introspection. Seek one thing alone: to purify your love of God more and more, to abandon yourself more and more perfectly to His will and to

love Him more exclusively and more completely, but also more simply and more peacefully and with more total and uncompromising trust.

If you are sincere in following this path you will be glad to welcome the trials and crosses God sends you and although they may cause intense and baffling pain to your soul you will take them in all peace and meekness and interior joy, realizing the love that comes with them from God and resting in the assurance that He is using these instruments to restore His likeness in you more and more perfectly.

Sanctity and contemplation are only to be found in the purity of love. The truly contemplative soul is not one that has the most exalted visions of the Divine Essence but the one who is most closely united to God in faith and love and allows itself to be absorbed and transformed into Him by the Holy Ghost. To such a soul everything becomes a source and occasion of love.

"Even as the bee extracts from all

plants the honey that is in them and has no use for them for aught else save for that purpose, *even so the soul with great facility extracts the sweetness of love that is in all things that pass through it.* IT LOVES GOD IN EACH OF THEM, WHETHER PLEASANT OR UNPLEASANT." (Spiritual Canticle, xxvii.)

To such a soul the pleasant or unpleasant accidents of things and events gradually fade away and disappear from sight. The only thing that matters is to please the Beloved and since in all things we can please Him by appreciating the love He sends to us in them, the contemplative finds equal joy in the pleasures and pains of mortal existence, in the sorrows as well as the delights of daily life. "For the soul knows naught but love and its pleasure in all things and occupations is ever the delight of the love of God." *(Ibid.)*

St. John of the Cross uses strong words to tell us the value of contemplation: "Let those that are great actives and think to girdle the world with their outward works take note that *they would bring far more profit to the Church and be far more pleasing to God if they spent even half this time in abiding with God in prayer* . . . Of a surety they would accomplish more with one piece of work than they now do with a thousand and that with far less labour." (Spiritual Canticle, xxix, 3.)

And he adds:

"A very little of this pure (mystical) love is precious in the sight of God and of greater profit to the Church than are all works together." *(Ibid.)*

THE DANGER OF QUIETISM

The words of St. John of the Cross must be understood in the context of the saint's own life. He was not preaching an absolute repudiation of all duties and responsibilities and all works and labours for the Church of God or for other men. He and St. Theresa of Avila, the greatest contemplatives of their time, were also very active and laboured and suffered much for the reform of the Carmelite Order. But the meaning of St. John's argument is this: activities prompted by our own tastes and judgements and ambitions and ideas will be riddled with imperfection and will always tend to disturb the union of our soul with God. On the other hand, God desires to bring us to this perfect union with Him *in order that our minds and wills, perfectly united and absorbed in Him, may act in perfect harmony and coordination with Him, as free instruments of His*

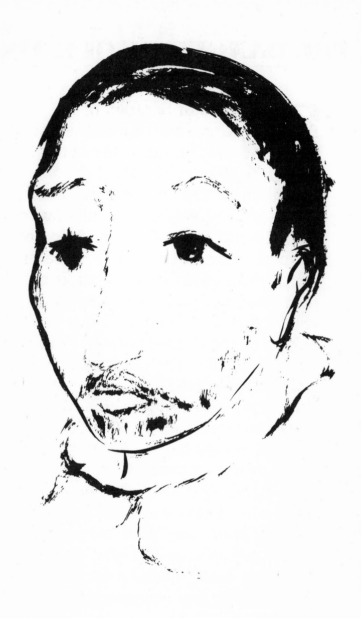

love and mercy. Thus He uses contemplatives to communicate His love to other men.

The heresy of quietism, on the other hand, encloses a man within himself in an entirely selfish solitude which excludes not only other men but even God Himself.

Quietism, while bearing a superficial resemblance to Christian contemplation, is actually its complete contradiction. The contemplative empties himself of every created love in order to be filled with the love of God alone, and divests his mind of all created images and phantasms in order to receive the pure and simple light of God directly into the summit of his soul. The quietist, on the other hand, pursuing a false ideal of absolute "annihilation" of his own soul, seeks to empty himself of *all* love and *all* knowledge and remain inert in a kind of spiritual vacuum in which there is no motion, no thought, no apprehension, no act of love, no passive receptivity but a mere blank without light or warmth or breath of interior life. Thus the quietist imagines that he is being passively moved by God.

Christian contemplation, being produced in the soul by the most sublime and delicate action of infused love, makes the soul perfect in the love of God while perfecting all the other virtues in that same contemplative love. But to the quietist the quest for virtue is "self-love" and the desire of heaven is also "self-love." The hope of union with God in heaven is considered mercenary. The desire to practice virtue and avoid sin is regarded as an "imperfection" because it supposedly troubles the "peace" of the "annihilated" soul.

Christian contemplation is the perfection of love and quietism is the exclusion of all love. Actually it is the quintessence of selfishness, because the quietist encloses himself in his own shell and keeps himself in a torpor in order to shut out all the painful realities of life which Christ would have us overcome by love and faith and

Christian virtue.

The "prayer" of the quietist is no prayer at all because the mind and will are entirely inert and dead: that is to say, they remain completely inactive while a constant stream of distractions and temptations is allowed to pour through them passively without the slightest show of effort to counteract them by conscious attention to God or to anything else.

If your contemplation is a complete blank or a mere spiritual chaos, without any love or desire of God, then be persuaded that you are not a contemplative. But on the other hand, remember that in the beginning of contemplation as well as in times of great trial, the desire and awareness of God are something so deep and so mute and so tenuous that it is hard to realize their presence at all. However, a glance is sufficient to tell you that they are there. In fact, the true contemplative suffers from the fact that he thinks he is without desire of God: and that very fact bears witness to his desire. This suffering itself is often the work of infused love. Therefore the Christian contemplative, even when he fears that his prayer is hopelessly sterile and useless and distracted, contradicts his own fears by the very intensity of *the anguish with which he longs for God.* If you feel that anguish and longing, be satisfied that you are not a quietist. Continue to seek God in love and self-abasement, and you will find Him.

Do not think, therefore, that in order to avoid quietism you must force yourself to meditate and produce acts and affections when this has become practically impossible. On the contrary, that would be fatal to God's work in your soul, if the signs of contemplation described above are verified in you. Be content to remain in loneliness and isolation and dryness and anguish waiting upon God in darkness. Your inarticulate longing for Him in the night of suffering will be your most eloquent prayer and will be more valuable to you and to the Church and

will give more glory to God than the highest natural flights of the intelligence or the imagination. But be persuaded, on the contrary, that God is here working to raise your intellect and will to the highest perfection of supernatural activity in union with His Holy Spirit. By pouring His Wisdom into your soul He is accomplishing the greatest work of His love and forming the perfect likeness of Christ, His incarnate Word, in you and perfecting His Church through everything that you allow Him to perform by the agency of your free will transformed and elevated in Him. Praise and glorify God, you who have tasted the first fruits of his marvelous grace, and pray to Him to continue His great work in your soul. Withdraw yourself from all care, trust not in yourself but in Him, do not be anxious or solicitous to perform great works for Him until He leads you Himself by obedience and love and the events which His Providence directs, to undertake the works He has planned for you and by which He will use you to communicate the fire of His love to other men.

This is the great work of His Love which is designed to overthrow the powers of the world in the moment of their seeming triumph. This is the great work of Love which will be performed in many obscure and weak and unknown men and women, Christians despised by the world and cast aside as useless: men suffering in prisons and concentration camps, women starving in the bombed cities of the world, labourers, poor farmers, humble priests, nuns in convents, simple lay brothers, mothers of families, and even little children. In these souls Christ will enkindle in the latter days of the world the fire of a great charity to counteract the love that has grown cold in the souls of the Lords of the earth.

Father and Maker of Love, dwelling within our hearts in inaccessible Light, together with Thy Son, send forth the seven Gifts of the Holy Spirit into our souls. Purify our minds not only of sin but of all the vanity of earthly wisdom and make us the docile instruments of Thy all-Holy Will in simplicity and truth, that the brightness of Thy Son Jesus may shine in our lives and give Thee glory.

Veni Domine Jesu! Amen.